The Invisible God

The Invisible God

Poems for Devotions

John J. Brugaletta

RESOURCE *Publications* · Eugene, Oregon

THE INVISIBLE GOD
Poems for Devotions

Copyright © 2017 John J. Brugaletta. All rights reserved. Except for brief quotations in critical publications or reviews, no part of this book may be reproduced in any manner without prior written permission from the publisher. Write: Permissions, Wipf and Stock Publishers, 199 W. 8th Ave., Suite 3, Eugene, OR 97401.

Resource Publications
An Imprint of Wipf and Stock Publishers
199 W. 8th Ave., Suite 3
Eugene, OR 97401

www.wipfandstock.com

PAPERBACK ISBN: 978-1-5326-1848-2
HARDCOVER ISBN: 978-1-4982-4408-4
EBOOK ISBN: 978-1-4982-4407-7

Manufactured in the U.S.A.

For the Reverend Canon Mark Shier

"He is the image of the invisible God,"
Colossians 1:15

Contents

4. Desires and Deceptions

5. Church

6. Messages through Our World

7. Translations

Acknowledgments

The poems listed below were previously published in the journals indicated, sometimes in a slightly different form.

A Civil Reply to Screwtape	*The Lamp-Post*
Ballade of the Hanged Men	*TRINACRIA*
Church	*Time of Singing*
Consummations	*Blue Unicorn*
Hope	*Blue Unicorn*
No Breaking Branch	*The Lyric*
Sun	*Blue Unicorn*
The Speed of Light	*Chronicles*
Three Translations from Dante	*South Coast Poetry Journal*

1. Quests

"Seek and you will find, knock and it will be opened to you."

LUKE 11:9

"Without the quest, there can be no epiphany."

CONSTANTINE E. SCAROS

THE BLIND ONES

If the bard in the Odyssey is a clue,
Homer himself was blind
but saw so clearly the Achaean ships,
the spears apparently slow in gutting a man,
the effete Trojans at their tower,
that we see them through his absent eyes.

Tiresias too, perhaps more than a fiction,
saw more than the sighted,
the running sore hidden at the heart
of Thebes, the parricide, the incest
to which others were blind until
the blindest of them all tore out his eyes
so he would see no more his offenses,
and then finally saw most truly of all.

Milton certainly, Paul as well.

And so we close our eyes to kiss,
and when we savor some delicious food,
and when we sleep to dream, perhaps of You,
and when we speak to You in darkness,
hands shielding our eyes, blinded for minutes,
hoping to catch a glimpse of You.

A CIVIL REPLY TO SCREWTAPE

> *"[God] has made change pleasurable to them. . . .*
> *But since He does not wish them to make change. . .*
> *an end in itself, He has balanced the love of change*
> *in them by a love of permanence."*

THE SCREWTAPE LETTERS

I love a change of pace, a change of scene,
But when I've lost my way among the new,
I find the same old thing makes me serene.

A flat stability is much too clean;
I long to rove, to taste, to live askew
And love the change of pace, the change of scene.

But then adventure soon becomes obscene;
I trade the seascape for my kitchen's view,
Because the same old thing makes me serene.

You demons bait your hook with flash and sheen,
And scheme to net and land and kill us through
Our love for change of pace, for change of scene.

But heaven's planted here a sweet routine
Of table, of our bed, and of a pew.
We know these same old things make us serene.

Our saving grace is that we live between
Those ancient trees and these that lately grew.
We love a change of pace, a change of scene,
But only in the old are we serene.

LITTLE FLAME

Here I tend on bended knee
    This uncertain tiny light,
Coaxing it with twigs and breath
    Till it shatter cold and night.

Should it grow so I can see
    Where to walk and where to rest,
I may sweep and order here
    For the coming of our Guest.

I had sensed the pits and bones;
    Firelight tells me nothing new,
Only steeping my shut eyes
    In the miserably true.

If this little flame will grow,
    He may come to grace my day,
So the breath that helps it climb
    Blows in words with which I pray.

QUEST OF THE MAGI

Nothing is true below the moon;
    Only the stars are wise.
That's why we blink at things of earth,
    Searching the steadfast skies.

Once we'd observed the rising star,
    Each from his proper land,
Three of us took a mount and food,
    Met as if all were planned.

On went the star, and we went on
    Following where it led.
Give no belief to those who say
    Truth will elude the head.

We had no sense where God's Son lay;
    All we pursued was truth.
When we were there, we found our goal
    Lodged in a kind of booth.

Down we dismounted, knelt and gave
    Frankincense, gold and myrrh.
Herod demanded we report,
    But we did not concur.

We then returned to our homelands,
    Better for having gone,
All of us changed by truth we'd seen:
    Light of the coming dawn.

MATURING

Each day means fewer things that he can do.
Some years ago he lost his sense of smell,
and now he hardly bends to tie his shoe.

You understand. I'm sure that you can tell
he's getting old, he's edging toward his grave.
Slave traders aren't enticed; he wouldn't sell.

I won't say he is cowardly or brave—
he's just uninterested in pain or fear.
He's lived from birth inside an autoclave.

But now his heart is cooked, his eyes are blear,
and he has seen some things he'll never say,
except by tangents, from this biosphere.

One thing he still delights in is to play
while kneeling with the children as he'd pray.

BIRTHPLACES OF IMMORTALITY

Cities and hamlets that lay wherever the Greeks
pronounced their Hellenic language claimed
to be birthplace and home of the father of poets, great Homer:
Chios, Salamis in Cyprus, Ionia, Smyrna,
and even Egyptian Thebes. But a man can be born
in a single location alone, and so one speaks true,
while the others are wishful pretenders who wink at the truth.

So do the tumbled adorings of India lie,
and the horse and the flame of the Persians, the disengagement
of Buddha in China, the worship of trees and of animals,
Arabic efforts to bolster their racial esteem—
lies to acquire for themselves the home-place of God.
But He broke into time at a single location, a Man,
perturbing the ones who, if able, had sent Him back home.

THE CAMEL AND THE NEEDLE'S EYE

The rich young man speaks

I have more sheep and goats, more houses, slaves
than Job before disaster laid him low.
My wife is out of Solomon and bears
a stair-step line of children to my fame.
But here and there I see a boil upon
the smooth skin of my life, a sign that all
may one day, in a sudden wind, collapse
and leave me naked, unprotected, shamed.

I woke some nights ago and felt the hands
of doubt, of indecision, of my youth
that gripped my neck and told me I am small.
When dawn returned (how long the night can be)
I checked my wealth and saw fragility.
So when I heard a teacher was nearby
I went to him and caught Him on the point
of leaving us. I wanted some assurance
that my acts, which held to Moses' law,
were adequate to buy eternal life.

He seemed at first to ratify my goal
by listing those commands I had obeyed.
But when I said I'd kept them all my life,
He saw the wall of safety I had built
around my life: my wealth, my comfort, shield
against humiliation and decay,
and laid his hand of discourse on those bricks.
Allow me here to tear it all away,
He said, and follow me to deathlessness.

At once I saw myself as stripped and shown
for children's entertainment and for fools.
I saw myself again a shameful child,
embarrassed, disrespected and debased.
These crumbs of good, I thought, had kept me warm
thus far. Why lose this good to grasp at one
that was a promise only, one man's word?
So I declined and went back to my keep
and sat among my rotting palisades.

I later heard the Romans nailed Him dead,
but He revived. If that proves true, I'm lost.

THE EDGE OF LIGHT

A clearing in old growth,
a campfire at its hub,
our tents pitched all around
along the edge of light.
We lay in sleeping bags,
some telling tales
to push the dawning near
the threat of darkened woods.

The stories went around
until we mostly were
agreed that some had shed
new light upon the fire—
redundancy of course.
Some lay along the edge,
while others went too far
into the baffling dark
for us to understand,
and so brought in more dark.

We've moved our tents away
at almost every dusk
to know more of what used
to be the trackless dark.
But some still love the dark
because it seems to them
that it will make them free.
We've had no word from them,
only their gargled pleas.

OUR WAIT FOR THE MESSIAH

We must learn to reawaken and keep ourselves awake,
not by mechanical aids, but by an infinite expectation
of the dawn.

Henry David Thoreau

Like those who waited near where Jesus prayed,
we wait two thousand years and fall asleep.
"And yet we're blest; our lives are short," you say.
Ah but the promise fades, the prospect creeps.

Behind and forward of us stretches time
devoid of Him and of the way made straight.
Our churches try to keep and mime the Christ,
but only Christ himself bears glory's weight.

However, truth may be that Deity
desires in us a faith so large that we
will bear a stretch of seeming-endless wait
for Him, the Bridegroom, and our coming peace.

What good is knowing when He will come back?
Would we rise early then to fill our lamp oil's lack?

2. Assurances

"[Josiah] encouraged them in the service of the house
of the Lord."

2 CHRONICLES 35:2

"We desire each one of you to show the same earnestness
in realizing the full assurance of hope until the end."

HEBREWS 6:11

ASSURANCES

It's autumn (as the British say) when apples fall
blood-red against the whitened orchard floor,
each one an ineffective sun, too red, too small
for doing more than mime that middling star's one chore.

Enough of that. Those trees will blossom in the spring
and bear their succulence again, but we will not,
except in sons and daughters and their own offspring,
while we take to the soil to rest and then to rot.

Is there another life our souls will wake to find?
We have assurances there is, but then there are
assurances that nothingness awaits our mind,
as black and meaningless as space or fireplace char.

Where lies the fact? Is it where someone died and rose?
If people then were weak as we would be today,
they would not bet their lives on what they just suppose.
On that I'll base belief, and not on what some say.

THE SPEED OF LIGHT

A billion light years is a fantasy
to me and to a lot of other folks.
It ripples off the tongue like *meet for tea*
and many other words, including jokes.

But try to think of it in miles or feet.
How many trips to buy a shirt or shoes?
That speed your shot goes in a game of skeet—
the pellets are not fast at all. They ooze.

Before and after all our lives, the stars
explode, black holes collide and spread in trillions
while we eat breakfast, read a book, drive cars.
We live our tiny lives in modest millions.

Yet we, and maybe only we, observe
and think of it. Is that way we serve?

THE HAND

A box of matches is a homely thing,
a drawer that's movable in which there lies
a handy squad of soldiers sleeping cold.
But fumble one to hand and scratch its head,
and it will leap to life, an ardent plasma
avid to destroy a wooden world,
or light a candle's wick or else a stove.

It is no better and no worse than men
who love to build and also to destroy.
What is this cosmos but a field of gleams
that light a little while and then go cold?
What lives is temporal and loves to die.
And yet a trillion stars replace the dead.
Where is the hand that scratches their cold head?

THE BUNCH OF GRAPES AND THE SON

*The sun, with all those planets revolving around
it and dependent on it, can still ripen a bunch of
grapes as if it had nothing else in the world to do.*

GALILEO

The sun you see sets in the west and so
the west is where we sent our kings in death.
Is this back-logic, or directionless
reality that doesn't fit our sense
of one thing causing something else in time?

No matter. Grapes do need some sun to ripen
and every bunch of grapes is smaller than
our littlest world of loneliness and cold.

Now would grapes grow, think you, on Pluto's rock?
I think they would not. Yet the sun extends
invisibly an un-comedic hand
to hold it from an unsure, darkened fate.

And even comets (like the rarest guest)
will visit after cosmic intervals
to feel the clasping hand, then off again,
the prodigal who'll never stay at home.

HOPE

You have made us for Yourself, and our heart is restless till it rests in You.

St. Augustine

There's a hole in all of us
wider and deeper than time.
People often mistake it for a junkyard
and try to fill it with torn galoshes,
broken coffee mugs
and snaggle-toothed combs.
The hole accepts these,
but no one can ever find them again.

Then something seems to be
seeping into it
and slowly, too slowly to see,
it starts to fill itself.
Now and then it threatens to overflow.
That's when there's hope.
It's then that hope begins.

THE LEPERS

Because our skins are pocked,
because this renders us unclean,
because we do not wish to stain the pure,
we ring this warning bell and call, "Defiled."

We have no fellowship except
with those whose sickness shows like ours,
or did not till there came to us
the only man not leprous in the world.

He was immune to this.
It was his purity
that was contagious:
touched by him, we caught his good.

Those who stayed away
had leprosy like us
but hid it under silken ways.
And still they shun. They sicken yet.

THE GREATEST FRIEND

Do our beliefs evaporate with time?
A great man said that time is slower at
the beach than at the Himalayas' highest peak,
which I suppose would mean a miner's life
would be some minutes longer than if he
were living on the moon. I'd just as soon
stay here and build a shack down near the beach
and still believe one Man was truly killed,
then came to life, as thousands verified.

But minutes are not magic; time will not
persuade the cynic to use common sense.
For friends would leave; the rest would heap their scorn.
But better that than to ignore a Friend
who tuned the universe to make a home
for humankind, and also the unkind.

CONSUMMATIONS

The mind constructs a castle
Where only huts endure
And thinks the walking cleanly
That never knew a floor.

A mountain seems a spirit
Until it's underfoot—
Then any lowland forest
Pontificates on light.

Not so the final banquet—
More like the married pair
Who know the courting frenzy
More than they did before.

TO SEEK IS TO HAVE FOUND

He would not have inspired us to seek Him
unless we had already found him.

Thomas Merton

We seek I AM as bees seek scented blooms.
But bees are seeking nectar for their hive
and have already nectar nonetheless.
It's lack of recognition in closed rooms
that makes us search the fields, to scan and strive,
then find a church that promises to bless.

And when we feel that comforting surcease,
what shall we do but bow and kiss its lace?
For seeing Him would strike us blind as Paul.
Let's hope that's when a nephew or a niece
will help us toward that real and living Face.
Then we will know we've always felt its call.

He's with us on our journey to meet Him,
but until then our eyes are weak and dim.

3. Praying

"Pray to your Father who is in secret."

"[Prayer is] identifying oneself with the divine will by the studied renunciation of one's own."

PAUL CLAUDEL

IT MIGHT HAVE BEEN THE LOUVRE

It's no good going to the Met
To see a single painting and leave.
You're there, and so you stay,
And Delacroix, El Greco, Breughel, Braque, David
Pour every touch they'd mastered through your eyes.

At three o'clock, the walls grow tame;
No portrait, still life, landscape satisfies.
It's then some thoughtful face,
Completely prepossessed with art's pretentious work,
Makes mockery of all a hand can shape.

Allow it, graceful Father—grant
That when these apparitions fade, decline
To be delectable,
We'll turn our reddened eyes from images toward You,
And not to mock the rest, but vivify.

THE LANGUAGE OF PARADISE

Working on virtue is like learning a language.

N.T. WRIGHT

I think, great God, my acts of charity
will strew no blossoms on my path to You.
But surely Love is pleased when it's returned
in gratitude and in our learning how
to imitate your language fluently.
I speak it only haltingly for now,
but with your aid I hope to speak it true.
Let not my well-meant actions be so spurned
as to reveal a trust in You that's crude.

I am a child, my God, and babble much,
but You know all our tongues and understand
the native meaning of an infant's love.
I think perhaps our actions are like touch:
my head upon your shoulder tells You more
than airy words, and known by You above.

WITH THE SAVIOR

Without the Christ, what would this life be like?
A darkened room, no windows and no door.
The senseless repetition of a chore.
An ocean's flood without a hill or dike.

No stars or moon; an endless, pointless hike;
an evil tyrant spreading blood and gore;
all interests and all pleasure a dry bore;
each blade of grass as piercing as a pike.

Yet now we know a loving Father rules,
benevolent enough to make worthwhile
a dying sun and leaders who are fools.

We tolerate our neighbors and their guile.
We humor the recalcitrance of mules
with wisdom's patience and its hallmark smile.

SPEAKING WITH THE FATHER

Make us reliable my gracious Lord,
for we are still evasive, fickle, brash.
When we are wavering, give us your Word.
When we lack food, remind us of those fish.

How many lures there are that hook our lips
to keep us silent when we should refute.
How many times our thought will flag and lapse
until the time is gone and no one hears.

Give us, if it's your will, a steady core,
so that, if we are one day asked to speak
the tongue of heaven, we'll not stutter, ache,
wish we were fluent when nearby your throne.

CHEATER'S PRAYER

Lord, preserve the superficial.
It's so comfy and so sweet.
Ask for nothing sacrificial,
Though we'd like our lives complete.

We prefer our coffee pallid
And our loves a trifle cool.
Our beliefs might be invalid,
But they save us from misrule.

Give us days when our attention
Never is attracted by
Anything that merits mention,
Lest our self-esteem should die.

Should the real become too forceful,
We might grimace or perspire.
Give no cause to be remorseful.
Give us hymns. Give us a choir.

Let our well-worn formulary,
All its meanings rubbed away,
Exorcise the tough and scary.
Let our dim lamps bring us day.

If this world is but illusion
And a solider exists,
Saying so would breed confusion
And amuse the atheists.

Let our lives go on unruffled,
Smoothed by miracles, until
Noise and music both are muffled
By our unresisted will.

Should a coward's courage falter,
Him You pity and excuse.
Though we're braver, that should alter
Not a bit the rules You use.

We're all equal, say the sages,
So You must treat us the same.
Otherwise the Lord of Ages
Plays unfairly His own game.

Give us sunsets. Give us Bambis.
Never mind the mud and screams.
Don't think us Your namby-pambies;
Just remove our horrid dreams.

LOSING IS FINDING

In every town the corpses lie supine
down under sod where worms and microbes dine.
It's not a pretty thought when put that way,
but then they have another way to pray:
they're facing upward with their flesh forgot.
We perpendiculars could learn a lot
by contemplating how they contemplate.
They lose themselves in thought; they uncreate
that snagging robe of skin and then emerge
(one hopes) unsullied as a whim or urge
that suddenly is realized, takes hold
of them and shakes them better, like a scold,
but pleasanter, and friendlier. And then
they're set up on their youngish feet again
to see invisibilities head-on
now that their half-blind eyes are gone.

THANKS I

Your favors fall like monsoon rains around us,
making our lives possible through a temperate climate,
food and drink, an enjoyable biosphere, and people,
many of whom bear aspects one may delight in.

And for all this wealth, we return to You a word,
our thanks. It is even, now and then, spoken sincerely.
The indebtedness is so great as to be stifling,
and indeed many prefer to leave it unmentioned.

But perhaps the problem stems from a misconception
of gratitude, of its importance, not so much to You
as to ourselves, who through heartfelt gratitude to One
so generous as You, come to glimpse the leading edge
of what truly selfless giving may one day become in us.

THANKS II

Compassionate of You to let me walk
at this late season of my flimsy life.
Without that strength, penultimate perhaps,
I could not smile, enjoy, or speak of peace.
But half an hour of walking through the woods
becomes almost a dozen hours of love.

It's not a deal I ever bargained for;
I fear to haggle with the One who formed
this time for space, the tiny building blocks
of matter and the brains of porpoises,
of parrots and of chimpanzees, to say
but little of that marvel, human thought.

Yet I'm allowed to signal gratitude
for saving me from several ways to die
and from that death most horrible of all.

FROM THE WHIRLWIND

If You would speak to me as mortals utter words,
Resolve my puzzlements and clarify my world,
Tell me which party I should honor, which to shun,
Instruct me when to bellow, when to close my mouth,
Perhaps then I could walk through all my days in peace,
And everywhere I went I'd shed your healing light,
And You beside me whispering, "Do this, say that."

But when You speak, it's I who must reply to You,
And everything You ask reveals my ignorance,
And few things You award are what I had in mind.
It seems impossible to speak to One so vast,
But much more so when all my folly's understood
And You lean down to pour surprises in my ear.

NO BREAKING BRANCH

Let not this deluge of your careful gifts
contract my eye so tightly from your face.
What worse ingratitude than one who loves
the gift more than the giver's fond embrace?

It's true that, lacking these, we'd slowly die,
but lacking your affection, death would come
like sudden waves that wash away our world
and turn orations stutteringly dumb.

Give me enough for ease in my last days
as you gave me survival formerly,
but tempt me not with surfeiting, my God.
A branch too fruitful may destroy the tree.

BREAKAGES

Mantegna's frescoes in a thousand chips,
And that a tiny fraction of the whole.
The pilot who directed that one bomb
Had other things than frescoes on his mind.
And yet, a work the human spirit made,
A thing that lay beyond the feasible,
Is irretrievable, or nearly so.

And what of those we stabbed with witty phrase,
Their savings filched by barely legal schemes,
Their chastity destroyed, their loyalties
Encumbered, compromised, a lasting stench
Replacing what had rightfully been theirs.
Will Love and Wisdom in the afterlife
Restore those breakages and fill the gaps?

And if so, will the fillings glare as scars,
Retelling us forever what we broke?

CARITAS

They tell us, Lord, that You love to forgive,
especially when we have learned to live
enough like Christ to loathe a past mistake.
But what if when we hate it, still we make
the same one yet again? We cannot stand
the stench of us whose sins pretend they're bland,
yet etch away like acid who they are;
contagious ones who model, like a scar,
infections that will spread throughout the world
and leave our innocents extinct and furled.

We folks will worship what we daily view
in mirrors, think that it is really You.

And yet, and yet, You made us, and we speak;
we walk the earth, however we might reek.
Teach us who've made our modest, frail approach
that we ourselves are riding in a coach
traversing desert sands and finding there
a sullen, shifty beggar who will dare
to curse our ease—and we must then attempt
to give some water and a ride to this unkempt.

FABRICATIONS

Let me not ever utter yes to lies,
To pious fictions that engender hope.
I would not wring truth's neck until its eyes
Belie their witness in the microscope.

But let me neither stop my ears because
A story lays a basis for my peace.
We sniff when uncles quote their well-worn saws,
But use makes no validity decrease.

Give me such wisdom as to know by touch
A fabrication from a bedrock fact.
And if this last request is not too much,
Add courage to relay such truths intact.

Our God made language to convey what is,
But some make living an infernal quiz.

THE INVISIBLE GOD

Put out the sun and douse those other stars.
That cold, disorienting black could not
come near my desolation when You turn
your face and pass unspeaking on from me.
No breath but vacuums up the smell of death.
A thought will grimace, pale and disappear.

Give me, great Maker of existence, hope,
the will to stir myself to work—some gust
of pleasure for the world, that I may know
which colored crayons sketch out my request
to lip your name and then to strew your path
with tokens of esteem. Then when You turn
and leave me once again, I may recall
the clove scent of carnations when You smiled.

BEFORE BEING NOTIFIED

A word received: The King would come
    to see what I had grown.
I shaved my garden nearly bare
    and left one rose alone.

It was my best, the single bloom
    that I would have Him see.
For all the rest had spots, were chewed,
    and spoke some ill in me.

But when He came, He praised the one,
    then asked for all the rest.
Confession: "They were maculate
    and this one was my best."

He said, "Before I came to have a look
I saw and plucked them from your living book."

HERETICS

How many soldiers You have had, my God,
who went to battle for what they perceived
to be the facts concerning who You are.
Some were defeated, relegated now
to handbooks on the history of faith,
while others wrote compellingly, and so
are lionized as heroes of your church.

Subdued by violence or politics, they
felt that they defended You. Uplift them and
subject them not to Hades' gibbering.
Correct them if they erred; if they were right,
give them a robe and ring if it's your will,
and taste their praises in a hidden church.

PRAYER ON GOING TO BED

Bolt our doors of apprehension, Spirit,
As we relinquish reason and recline.

Be You within, that toothed and leering sprites
May fear and pass unharmed our sleeping souls.

We're forced to sleep, and sleep to witness dreams,
But let them harmless come, though meaningless.

Grant also, Breath of God, that, with our strength,
Our wills may be refreshed to live in peace.

Tomorrow come, allot the day some task
That wakes a smile upon the Father's lips.

"MY KINGDOM IS NOT OF THIS WORLD"

John 18:36

That's good, Lord, because this world
is not one that would please You,
what with earthquakes, volcanoes,
tsunamis, disease and predators.

There are, of course, our feeble attempts
at imitating your kingdom.
And there are periods
of peace, even the external kind,
but when they end, the ship of
this world comes close to wreckage
on the rocks of greed, vengeance
and all the forms that unearned pride
will take—abuse of power and the lust
to make all others into minions.

But still we wait for You,
some of us working as careful stewards.
For You said You'll return one day.
But when, Lord, when?

4. Desires and Deceptions

"Not that I desire the gift; but that I seek the fruit which increases to your credit. I have received full payment."

PHILIPPIANS 4:17-18

"Let no man deceive you with vain words."

EPHESIANS 5:6

DESIRES

The things we feel we need to have
one day will fade in our esteem.

In youth it was a pocket knife
or doll that cried and wet itself.
In teens it was a car that ran,
however many squeaks it spoke.

With age the sexes are reversed:
the women want their youth again;
the men desire a doll that smiles.
In fact they both long for their youth;
the difference is, when they were young
they yearned for things they might receive.

What's left when petty wishes die?
What longing dreams disturb our sleep?

THE HEADWAITER AT CANA

When first I sipped from what the groom had brought,
it came to me how poor he was, and that,
translated, said my fee was more than he
could bear, so I resigned myself to just
a pittance of my customary fee.

As one last jug of wine was almost dry,
the servants brought out several more to me.
And this new batch, compared with what we'd had,
was as a royal gem to common stone.

The guests were tipsy from the sour wine.
How could they taste, and how appreciate,
this subtle but delicious quaff? I voiced
my puzzlement at his reversing of
tradition's hospitality, and yet
his answer never reached my careful ear.

When all of them had stumbled home in something
toward an ecstasy, a servant told
how one impressive guest had turned the full
capacity of water to that most
delicious wine. So I suppose that untaught
explanation must at last suffice.
But I suspect the host was not as poor
as I'd supposed. Yet still the serving order
is a puzzlement. Oh well, it's not
as though such oddities do not occur.

ACCOUNT BALANCING

She calls the bank each morning,
    Her checkbook in her hand,
To hear recorded voices say
    How her finances stand.

She spent two hundred on some shoes,
    Deposited her pay,
Then spent some more, deposited—
    So what's the sum today?

It's earn a bit, and use it soon
    To buy a little thrill,
Which lasts a little while, and then
    There comes another bill.

But when she wakens in the dark
    Then everything comes clear.
She recollects a drunken moth
    And vastness of this sphere.

JACOB VS. DAVID

*Her sins, which are many, are forgiven,
for she loved much.*

LUKE 8:47

Mysterious the way He picked a man
who tricks his father and Esau as well,
then doubles down the fraud on Leah's dad.
We're never told that he repents, for when
he gifts Esau, his prompt is merely fear.

And David, "after God's own heart," recalls
at every section of his life but one
that God exists, God sees, God favors good,
especially the good of self-control
when lust will itch and most of us will scratch.

But most mysterious of all is how
the stricter members of our family
assume the lifelong sins of Jacob are
a thing we must forget, while David's urge,
in budding spring, is unforgivable.

Admittedly he had the Hittite killed,
but then repented after Nathan's tale.
Would David's son refuse then to forgive
a man whose motivation was his love?
And not alone erotic love, I think,
but love that lasted all God's hero's life.

PRODIGAL FRIEND

When all my friends are busy or estranged,
the telephone and email screen asleep,
I sit alone and think of you, my God,
and unresenting, you grant audience.
In fact, if parables speak true, you like
my crass return so much you cup your ear
to listen carefully to every word
I sputter in my shameful last resort—
like it so much you probably prepared
my solitude. And recognizing that,
I hold at last my token gift for you,
my gratitude for this confinement that
reveals the source of all the joy I take
in mortal voices, earthly hand-cupped ears.

WILFULNESS

Be not so dainty over our free will,
but if You grant my current prayer, I beg
that You then make my will like yours;
for I have seen insanities that men make
when "Freedom" is their call, and chaos comes.

Let me be free to choose, and I might pick
the coarsest knave, the dullest simpleton
to lead me in response to love of home,
or in response to what my homeland was,
or even in nostalgia's mindless grip.

Give me—give *us,* the wisdom You possess,
but not in full, I plead. Our minds cannot
compact what nestles in your own. Take care
that our thin skulls do not explode in zeal
to be as You, which was our fall's one cause.

AGAPE CHAMPION

What insolence, to ask if I can love.
Of all those you might ask, you come to me?
I, who teach the others by the way
I live, my arms spread wide for that embrace
the sage apostle said to give our friends?
My face will ache when I relax at home,
the thorn that follows days of rosy smiles.

And everyone I love I then forgive,
and then forgive again when they return
my love with snide remarks and filth in words.
Four hundred ninety times the Lord commands
we wipe remembering's painful slate of those
offending us. My worst offender gave
two hundred forty-two. I still forgive.

I would not like to think of his demise,
the boiling pitch up to his nether parts,
huge hornets stinging lips and eyes, the roar
of hard-rock music always in his ears.
No, I should like to see him smiling when
at last he sees the love that passed him by.
It's that I pray for, that I beg to see.

Assuming you're aware my Emma's gone,
you must have heard how loud I wept.
She cooked, she cleaned. It's true she criticized,
but that's all right. I grinned and shrugged it off.
I hardly think of it these days at all.
I wept for love, and just before she went,
I said to smile and took her photograph.

I made her happy, that much I can prove.
Her smile reflected love I always gave.

THE INCARNATE ONE HIMSELF

You want to walk the dusty roads with Jesus,
talk with him about your rheumatism,
ask him why your newborn daughter died,
make suggestions as to things He said
that trouble you, that just sound wrong.

And then you watch him stand and puzzle out
an answer to the woman and her crumbs.
You sniff the odor of a man on a hot day.
You notice that, on a boat, He sits on a cushion.
You see lice in his hair, uncut toenails,
dirty hands at a meal, sharp words to lawyers.

Do you still wish to be near, to know him?
Or would you rather meet him on a clean page,
in an archaic translation, with footnotes?

MAKING PREDATORS

The world is rich with hamsters, rats and mice,
the vegetarians whom Dr. Spock
envisions as the future racial stock:
Industrious, bucolic, little, nice.

We see them nibbling barley, nuts and rice.
But look where coiled and mottled as a rock,
one hopes to slip his body like a sock
down over head and hips—a meal concise.

And you, my friend—with Beemer, houses, cash,
no more ideal than you are small and cute—
create the dragon on your gleaming stash.

This is no wish for harm. I pray the brute
will starve and you get nothing worse than rash.
But history's a slut, and so is loot.

SUN

Despite these clouds, we know the sun is there
somewhere behind, a memory, and distant.
But knowledge is not all, as you're aware,
and so our source of light is non-existent.

How shall we live if everything is dead?
It's always late in fall this kind of day
when all the world is dying in our head.
What joy is there if all things must decay?

If I could blow those clouds away, I would.
But would you be the happier for that?
I'd like to think you would. I know you should.
It may be no more loathsome than a chat.

I'll take the chance. The sun has not absconded.
And how unlikely: You and it have bonded.

5. Church

"To the angel of the church in Ephesus: . . . I have this against you, that you have abandoned the love you had at first.

REVELATION 2:1-4

"[Churches are] nothing but a section of humanity in which Christ has really taken form"

DIETRICH BONHOEFFER

CHURCH

The little country church is painted white,
White as the snow around it this cold day,
And so its heavy iron bell must play
A shadowed sound across the blinding light.

But in the church a woodstove blushes hot,
As do the saved, embarrassed by their past,
Contrasting with this good beyond their caste,
As if they'd won a mansion or a yacht.

So there the upright Baldwin belts a hymn
As colorful as awe and skills allow,
Each woman like a blossom-laden bough,
The trunk-like husbands dressed in gray, and trim.
The world is cold, demands a face that's grim,
But still the church is warm, at least for now.

AFTER THE SERMON

Sunday evening.
Your ears ring with the assurances.
Then the week-long march downhill
past the daily devotionals
and past the paper cups and graffiti
of an entertainment-mad world.

Where are the handrails
to keep us from the cliffs?
Who can understand
the chitter of the hummingbird,
the huff of the black-bear sow,
the billion voices of the earth?

Yet somewhere you will find
notations on last Sunday's homily,
and just in time. It's Saturday.
They are like photographs in sepia,
pallid representatives of wisdom
interlaced with love.

CHURCHGOING

Tomorrow is a Sunday morning
and once again the switched-on smiles,
assurances that we are not gnashing
our teeth on the frailties of others.
Again the sense that the Father
is pleased by our being here at all,
but would prefer we sang and prayed
with Him in mind.

Again we sit expecting entertainment,
a play on Word, something understood,
a note of mystery, Eleusinian perhaps,
displaying us as having died and now
risen with a jolt of liveliness,
making us feel we could fight off any foe,
huge python or atheist,
and live like a pagan hero to boast of it.

A little better to go home afterward,
consider the blessing of our spouse
and offer our gratitude to the Lord.

THE AFFECTIONATE VILLAGE

The gathering is small at any time,
but in August those not on vacation
are few. The pastor preaches on the
City of God, asking why not the
Village of God. No answer. No idea.

Yet there they are, one hand's worth,
all of them different as horses and cats,
yet fascinated with, and careful of,
one another, a small *polis* in Pericles' day,
a clan with no blood ties, or few.
Confidences pass among them
like bees in a rose garden.

But love that flourishes in a city is like
hummingbirds surviving on the polar tundra.

RESET GEM

Someone found a diamond,
a huge and lustrous thing.
It formulated light,
made it visible music.

The salesmen set it
in ordinary gold
with lesser gems.

But the gold wore thin,
and the everyday jewels
fell in the dust.

Still they kept the diamond,
reset it in silver,
a plain foil
for a precious stone.

When the silver tarnishes,
others will set it in bronze,
until one day its irons crack
and it will be known as Hope.

TEMPLE

Though it was stone, it was a type of heart,
receiving lifeblood from the land and work
and pumping it through an aorta back
to Him, the Mind, the Uncontainable.

But like most bodies it possessed a skin,
an outer limit to its functioning,
keeping out Samaritans and Romans.
And this the Mind, their God, forbade with force.
This was the message in the knotted cords,
the shocking spanking and the warning words.

But every living thing desires to live
and keep itself like immortality
and is prepared to kill just to survive,
maintaining purity it hardly kept.

SUNDAY MORNING

The oak pews are empty,
too early for people to arrive.
But the worn places and scratches are honorable.
They are ready to receive more of
the timid, watchful girls and their restless brothers,
the casual adults in their jeans,
the older men in coats and ties,
and the octogenarian ladies in sweaters.

The flowers on the altar have been given
in memory of someone most have never met.
A professional florist would not be satisfied,
but everyone who comes will think them fine.

Singly and in pairs the members amble in,
never quite filling the place.
Then the piano reminds us of the rustic tune,
and the voices, unsure, trembling,
rise up like a flock of birds,
always intending to reach the sky
but never realizing how far away it really is,
never realizing, either, that the gesture is enough.

CHURCH PEWS

It's Sunday now and time to wash and shave,
Then go to where attendees all behave,
At least while they are on the holy grounds.
The clock says, "Time," the virtual bell sounds,
And we arrive where people act so odd
It almost proves existence of their God.
We sit as audience, but then participate,
Sing songs that rank as second or third rate,
Recite a creed we sometimes can't believe,
Are urged to deeds we hardly will achieve,
Or feel ourselves made holy by osmosis.
Outside a church, it would be called neurosis.

But something in the walls, and those they hold,
Makes all of us particularly bold
To bare what we would otherwise keep hid
A meter deep and sealed tight with a lid.

GIFTS OF THE SPIRIT

Some run the buzzing vacuum, some a cloth
To polish oaken pews until they gleam;
One hand will water rhododendron trees,
Another digs to plant azaleas,
While in the office someone types and files
And takes the interrupting call with ease,
And someone else replaces bulbs that light
The place where we give ringing thanks for light.
Around a table sit the councilors
Adjudicating where finances go,
While several household kitchens make the air
Delicious with the smells of stews and loaves
For hungry worshippers on Wednesday nights.
Some wash and press the snowy altar cloth,
While others see that there is wine and bread.
Some carry logs to pile and set aflame,
Making the fireplace bright, the faces warm,
While others fill the urn for coffee cups.

From different parts of town the greeters come
And stand outside the doors to welcome in
Familiar faces and some searching ones;
From different parts the punctual ushers come
To take the offerings and tally them.
Some make the organ speak or call in zeal,
Or the piano strike its tensioned cords,
Releasing pent-up music on the air.
Then those who sing like morning birds are heard,
And those of us who sound like barnyard hens
Admix our tinny voices to the song,
Which heaven alchemizes to bright gold.

Then someone leaves her pew and reads to all
Some passages from that immortal Book.
And then the Pastor's voice speaks to his sheep,
Who recognize its tones and stand alert;
The news is good—they strain to hear each word.
And then the sermon, gloss upon the text,
A guided meditation on the Word,
A loving blend of thought and urgency.

Soon worshippers go altarward to eat
And drink as Christ's apostles did
That fatal night the world devoured his life,
The pastor's hand distributing the bread,
Some others sips of lifeblood from the grape.
In other rooms the children sit and hear
Of Samson's hair and David's sling, and how
Our Lord invited children to approach.

All these add what ability does best,
The drum or tuba to the symphony,
The wiring, pipes and windows of a house.
Although the wires are live, the pipes are full,
The windows let in light, no frowning porter
Guards the door to keep us few in joy,
But ventures out to bring the wayward in,
For still the Wedding Feast has empty chairs.

REAL PRESENCE IN THE EUCHARIST

(Judas speaks)   John 13:26-27

He said it was his body that He held,
but clearly it was ordinary bread.
And after eating, once again He said
the wine was part of Him, this time his blood.
Both seemed akin to parables He'd told:
a children's tale of kings and servants with
a pithy lesson squeezed from his wives' tale.

But back to wine. He added at the end,
"Do this in memory of Me." I thought,
"A puzzling thing to say. Was it his blood
or a memorial? If truly blood,
it must be stricken from the mind for sons
of Abraham. If plain memorial,
the sip or draft might prompt the mind a bit,
but not the eyes and ears. So odd," I thought.

A little later in the meal, He took
a shred of bread and dipped it in the wine,
then motioned that the sop was meant for me.
It took me by surprise, for I'd been musing
on a certain thirty shekels, so
I wrenched my mind away, and for a bit
I thought the sop, then back again to silver.

The wine-soaked bread was down my throat and I
could feel a viper strike me in the chest.
It was for me no memory of Him,
but of voracity that fed upon
my soul, my spirit, all my desires—my life.

In time I saw this wretchedness would stay.
I purposed then to end my life, and saw
as well his bread and wine invited good
or evil, God or Satan, life or ruin.
If only I had seen how loving was
the sop that offered me a rich forgiveness
if only I had kept my mind on Him
instead of on my plans to take him off.

DOWN THE LINE

Here I am, Lord, nothin' fancy,
    Just a man that drives a truck.
Lived a life that's awful chancy,
    Always countin' on my luck.

Luck give out in Kansas City,
    Lost my truck and near my life.
I ain't askin' for no pity.
    All I want's my kids and wife.

Here I am, Lord, tired and dirty,
    After I ain't prayed—let's see—
It's been twenty, maybe thirty
    Years since I been on this knee.

Just a mite of bread You're givin'
    And a drop or two of wine,
I'll go out and make a livin',
    Things'll work out down the line.

Now I'm back, things look some brighter.
    Faces all around here shine.
I can walk a little lighter.
    Things'll work out down the line.

A CRUSH ON LIFE

If I wanted to destroy all human goodness—
crush, as a man crushes an ant with his heel,
all of the feeding and healing and watching-in-pleasure—
I would smile a lot, smile till my face ached,
and I would talk always about loving others
and how we must forgive whatever they do,
even if it wasn't to us that they did it,
even if they plan to do it again to more people,
even if they use our automatic forgiveness
to twist souls, wrench privacies, crush possibilities.

I would say in low tones of seeming sincerity,
looking into their eyes one time and away another,
that good people never hate anybody or anything,
that love is all, a holding of everything to our breast,
even the rattlesnake—especially the rattlesnake.

THE WEDDING FEAST AT CANA

Although it covers one entire wall,
The guests and hangers-on spill out the sides,
For Veronese could not make it hold
The great, unruly number who, with Christ
In hearing, still would prattle of the food,
The chance of rain, migrating birds, or tell
The story of a bunion's agony.

They are, of course, a little drunk by now,
The host just tasting what a wine should be.
But no one's had a drink when we allow
Whole days to be consumed with choosing clothes,
Or training grass to do a carpet's job,
While somewhere in the house there sits the Man
Who stares unheeded deep within our eyes.

HEARING GOD

Among the stacks of books he gave away
Was one entitled *How to Hear Your God.*
His wife had bought them, seeking ways to pray,
To love, to see His face—she of the nod,

Or when awake, the single word, the smile.
He stows her walker when they've reached their pew,
Then sits himself beside her near the aisle
Where he can hear and nothing blocks her view.

The prayers and sermon pass her mind like air,
But she hears something; her attentive face
Is clear on that: initially the scare,
And then the strain to hear the tones in bass.

The books are useless now; they've sown their seeds.
We watch and see how He'll fulfill our needs.

6. Messages through Our World

"The Lord himself will give you a sign. Watch, a young woman shall conceive and bear a son, and shall call his name Immanuel."

ISAIAH 7:14

"'What sign have you to show us for doing this?' Jesus answered them, 'Destroy this temple, and in three days I will raise it up.'"

JOHN 2:18-19

A LITTLE BESTIARY*

A chickadee will fall
exactly like a leaf,
except that then
it rises to a branch again.

The leaf was once alive;
the bird will one day die.
But there's a gulf
between true flight and simple fall.

Such messages are in
the things that we pass by,
believing they
are merely there to be themselves.

HERODOTUS TELLS IT

fifth century B.C.

> *Stretching out His hand toward his disciples, He said,*
> *"Here are my mother and my brothers! For whoever*
> *does the will of my Father in heaven is my brother and*
> *sister and mother."*
>
> MATTHEW 12:48-49

Xerxes, king of Persia, was leading his vast army
to war when a rich Lydian offered his support:
2000 talents of silver and nearly four million gold Darics,
all of his wealth, he said. The king was so pleased that
he allowed Pythius to keep his wealth, and added to it.
He then made the Lydian his personal friend,
urging him to remain the generous man he was.

Later, as they neared battle, Pythius once more
approached the king and prayed he grant one favor.
"I have five sons, every one of them in your army.
I am an old man. Take pity and release my eldest
that he may take care of me and my possessions."

This infuriated the king. "You miserable creature!
I march in person with my own sons, brothers,
kinsmen and friends, I, the king. Yet you, a servant,
whom I allowed to keep his wealth and more,
whose duty it is to accompany me with every member
of your house, do you have the impertinence
to withhold your son from me?" And the king
gave orders that the son in question be split in half,
one half on each side of the road, that the army
may march between them, a kind of grim agreement.

It's an old story, yet it sounds so familiar, so meaningful.

CHRISTMAS TREE

We brought a tree home as a Christmas guest
and expected it to hold all our shiny baubles.
We handled its branches and needles, this alien
from another kingdom that we cut at the roots,
and it brought us its scent as a kind of love.

The fragrance of it spread to other rooms,
consecrating the curtains, blessing our attention,
removing any doubt that this was other-worldly,
this straining to please every friend and ourselves.

But then we lost our sense of smell, so now
what the scent did to us inwardly in our youth
is done without the tree, without its balm,
without its redolence waking and healing the air,
without nostrils, now only by the end result,
that exuberance, that joy, that complete happiness.

CLOSE SHAVE: A WESTERN

The killer lay back in the barber's chair,
His face in lather like a mad dog,
His neck exposed to the straight razor.
The barber knew of the good men killed,
The widows left with their hungry young,
Those young who were left, their throats uncut.
The others will never say what he did
While their mothers watched in the ransacked house.

So the razor hung in the air above
The throat the girls had seen at close range.
But the killer knew, and he smiled to know
That a man will live with a bleeding throat
Just long enough to draw and fire,
And he knew the barber knew it too.
So the barber shaved the killer's face,
Who paid him nothing and left with a sneer.

Precious few men will die to end
The anguished deaths of homespun folk.

THE NURSERY ARRANGED

No one has ever heard the harmony
of turning spheres, and yet it seems they should,
so grandiose their motion seems they would
outsound the greatest portal's groaning swing.
Are they as oiled and slick as sleep? Or could
it be we're deaf to that full, constant ring?

It's neither, as I think the matter through,
for gas was coalesced and set to spin
as habitat for creatures as they grew
into the Maker's joy. If we should hear
their booming music it would peel our skin
and leave us pierced as gauze, as sheer.

They sound, and we would hear, but in the path
between their awful motion and our ears
the Father sets a hush. None but his wrath
would bring their noise to pulverize our sneers.

ELEPHANT AT OUR ELBOW

You're in a jungle hunting elephants.
Nearby, a tree trunk seems a rarity.
And then it budges and you realize
that you are standing just a foot away
from what you searched for with binoculars.

It was that way for eons with the earth.
We gazed and wondered at the Evening Star,
but had no notion that its sibling lay
beneath our feet in still proximity.
What else is much too large for us to see?

GOOD DREAM

He sent the human race what I call good dreams:
I mean those queer stories scattered all through
the heathen religions about a god who dies and
comes to life again and by his death, has somehow
given new life to men.

C.S. Lewis

On April 16, 1178 B.C., No Man
arrived home, having been away so long
the faithless said he certainly was dead.
But a seed he had planted before leaving
had matured of late, eager to
welcome him on his return, assuming always
the man would be recognizable.

His wife, all that remained
of his old and regal institution,
refused at first to receive him,
her reticence a show of judicious caution.
But returned he was,
and on this auspicious date,
proving and finding his lost identity
in each act simultaneously:
Athena's transformation of his looks,
the scar a boar left on his leg,
his bending of the impossible bow,
his intimate knowledge of the royal bed.

He grieved for all his subjects who must die,
no matter how they had deserved
more than the deluge of their blood.
A few, only a few, recalled
how generous a king he'd been.

His dog, like Simeon,
wagged his tail and died.

ESSAY ON DISORDER

It is the needlessness, more than the act,
that makes a fellow break a windowpane;
as with Augustine's pears, for which he had
no hunger, so the cheer was in the theft.

But some will say the cheer was need enough
for Faulkner's Flem, who cleaned the feces from
his boots onto a rich man's Persian rug.
Nice try, but then the cheer itself had come
from hatred, envy and revenge in him
who thought the feces fitting for his boss.

An appetite for chaos seems to lurk
within our souls, the fast disorder when
a booted foot comes down upon an ant.
And I suspect it emanates from that
primordial disorder that was left
when tumult was commanded into forms.
It was those forms, those shapes that we
and our terrarium proceeded from.
Consider Caliban, the island's gnome,
who lusts to rape the brave new world of youth.

If this is so, it argues that the wish
to have no government—no rules by which
we dance and till the land, marry,
raise our children, read, and laugh or kiss—
is suicide, the inclination toward
a nothingness destroying all we have.

This appetite, if left to breed, will be
the death of us and our long evolution
toward a civilized society.
It is, you know, our only way to joy.

LIKING IS DESIGN

How clever of the One, to make a bloom
Look red to us in making it attract
The sipping, pollinating flies and bees.
In tasting, they impregnate what seems good,
And propagate thereby a pretty world.

How all things wear a look of nonchalance
Quite purposely. In this way those who see
And thank the One who made them so are free
And not coerced to love, so love in fact.

LOVE VS. SALVATION

*Then after the morsel, Satan entered into
him. Jesus said to him, "What you are going
to do, do quickly."*

JOHN 13:27

Rugosa is a rugged kind of rose.
It shrugs off mildew and it stares down deer,
but this one wouldn't grow and so
I moved it where it had a lot more sun
and watered it and fed it mild amounts.

I love its old-man leaves,
its baby-finger blossoms,
its hips like cherries in the fall.

Though others grew and bore,
this one slouched.
Despite my tending and my love,
some quirk within it snuffed its will
to carry out inherited design.

I am truly sorry.
But when I've tried all possibilities,
it goes to compost,
leaving soil and sun for other things to grow.

MIRACLES

To found the era of the Law, the Lord
chastised a land with locusts in a cloud,
gave humble feet a path but drowned the proud,
commanded arid rocks so water poured.

To found the era of Good News, He fed
five thousand on a little bread and fish,
gave beggars more than they knew how to wish,
restored a Man to life who had been dead.

He seems to like beginning larger ages
by pouring miracles like needed rain.
If history's the book, God turns the pages;
He does so when He's ready for the next.
The paper rattles like a cosmic chain
and leaves us clever readers awed, perplexed.

TAP ROOTS

The redwoods and the firs
are flexing in the wind.
One tap root each demurs
to fall, because it's pinned

to earth by something deep
and out of human sight.
For death nearby will creep
and lure us into night.

As parables, they say
we must be anchored well
to live above the clay,
to breathe, consider, tell.

And then when we're blown down
we need a different root.
No specious smile or frown
will serve us as a suit

to save our fragile selves
from dark's indifferent shelves.

7. Translations

"It is better to have read a great work of another culture in translation than never to have read it at all."

HENRY GRATTON DOYLE

"[Translating is like] trying to pour yourself into an invisible glass so that you take the shape of your vessel and transmit the author's light and flavor."

NEVILL COGHILL

SONNET XXII BY MICHELANGELO

If my coarse hammer gives resistant stone
A human face, with brow and nose and lips,
It is my arm that guides it to create;
It borrows motion, cannot move alone.
But that Prime Mover, throned and still above,
Still makes Himself and others beautiful.
Just as no hammer can be made without
A prior hammer, that Life makes all alive.

And then, because a blow gains greater force
As it falls farther to the chisel's head,
A Hammer from the sky fell onto mine.
So mine will land without the slightest force
Unless impelled by that great Sculptor's arm,
Who, single handed, carved and shaped the world.

THREE EPIC SIMILES FROM DANTE'S *COMMEDIA*

Inferno

With all the storm and loud ferocity
of dogs attacking some poor begging tramp
who begs from where they stopped him in the yard,

the demons came from underneath the bridge
and swiped their pitchforks at my master's face.
He shouted sharp, "Be good, the pack of you.

Before you hook me with your little forks,
let one of you come close to hear me out,
and then, if nothing changes, do your worst.

Purgatorio

As birds that spend the winter on the Nile
will take to flight sometimes in wide formation
and then go single file for greater speed,

so did that crowd of hungry souls I saw
avert their faces, quicken their lean steps,
and speed away with single, keen desire.

Paradiso

The way a cloud will freeze and fall in flakes
of snow down through our air at Christmas time
(when Capricorn's about to touch the sun),

so did the sky adorn itself with flakes
that rose in clouds of those triumphant souls
who had remained below with us awhile.

I kept my sight on their resemblances,
and held it till the distance was so great
my seeing could not cross the air between.

BALLADE OF THE HANGED MEN

from the French of François Villon

You brothers who survive beyond our deaths,
   don't turn your thoughts so hard against our deeds,
   for if you sprinkle pity on our souls,
   God will pour his mercy on your heads.
You see us five or six still hanging here.
As for the flesh, we ate too much of it;
it's been long since devoured and decayed;
now see our bones, they turn to ash and dust.
No one who sees us rot should laugh at us,
   but pray to God that He absolve our sins.

Yes, we have called you brothers, but don't aim
   at us your scorn, though we were choked by rope,
   and justly so. In any case, you know
   how every man at times lacks common sense.
Plead for us—for we'll kill no one now—
to Him who is the Virgin Mary's Son,
that all His grace for us not blow away,
and that He hold us from hell's lightning bolt.
We now are dead; let no man show contempt,
   but pray to God that He absolve our sins.

The rains have washed away our blood and mud;
   the sun has dried our flesh and blackened us.
   Crows and magpies have fed on our eyes
   and plucked out all our beards and our eyebrows.
There's never been a time when we sat still:
first here, then there. It's like the fickle wind,
at its wild pleasure, jostles us non-stop,
more pecked and needled than a tailor's thumb.
So never dare to join our glum brigade,
   but pray to God that He absolve our sins.

Prince Jesus Christ, whose lordship's over all,
take care that Satan never rules this realm;
we have no interest in that fool today.
You men: I mean no touch of mockery.
Just pray to God that He absolve our sins.

AN ANCIENT COLLECT PARAPHRASED

Deus, qui nos in tantis periculis constitutos pro
humana scis fragilitate non posse subsistere, dona
nobis salvitatem.

O Lord, You know what fragile stuff we are,
For You it was who fashioned us like waves:
Blown into being somewhere out of sight,
We move until we break ourselves on earth.

The rocks surround us like a row of teeth;
All mean our death; they gnaw away our flesh.
This is the close terrarium You placed us in,
A grinning city filled with predators.

It cannot be that we will stand it long.
We have nowhere to turn but to our home.
O God, who crippled death, give us new lives.

www.ingramcontent.com/pod-product-compliance
Lightning Source LLC
Chambersburg PA
CBHW060421090426
42734CB00011B/2395